P9-DND-805

Découpage with Painted Backgrounds

Val Lade
&
Nerida Singleton

Sally Milner Publishing

First published in 1996 by
Sally Milner Publishing Pty Ltd
at 'The Pines'
RMB 54 Burra Road
Burra Creek
NSW 2620
Australia

© Val Lade & Nerida Singleton, 1996

Design by Anna Warren
Printed and bound in Australia by
Impact Printing, Melbourne

National Library of Australia
Cataloguing-in-Publication data:

Lade, Val.
Découpage with painted backgrounds

ISBN 1 86351 198 9

1. Découpage. I. Singleton, Nerida, 1948- . II. Title.
(Series: Milner craft series).

745.546

All rights reserved. No part of this publication may be reproduced,
stored in a retrieval system or transmitted by any means, electronic,
mechanical, photocopying, recording or otherwise, without prior
written permission of the copyright holders.

Introduction

In my workshops and seminars throughout Australia I have encountered many people in a similar position to my own — we do découpage, employing someone else's images, because we do not PAINT — or even draw. In no way could I wield an art brush and produce anything of value.

It occurred to me that we were all suffering from a lack of instruction, and that visual identification (or appreciation) of appropriate background painting techniques could be of enormous benefit to all découpage artists. I also thought that we needed some 'clues' to complementary designs for borders and backgrounds to use with our cut-out images. If we could be shown examples of images presented with different backgrounds, borders and decorations, they would open our minds to the possibilities.

When I met Val Lade five years ago she persuaded me that everybody could PAINT! Not with a brush, necessarily, but with a sea sponge. What a revelation!

Of course in my initial enthusiasm I purchased a full stand of paints, knowing absolutely nothing about mixing paint colour. Val found this highly amusing, wondering just how many shades of yellow one might need. We have conducted many workshops over the years and in each one Val concentrates on the importance of 'playing' with or experimenting with several colours, in differing quantities, to achieve different effects. You certainly don't need a full stand of paints!

I have browbeaten Val into participating in this book, to share her knowledge with us, which she always does so generously. She was given the task of producing four different backgrounds for six images, and two variations on a Christmas theme. These are truly magnificent examples she has given us, and they show clearly that changing the background changes the mood of our design, and can be subtle or dramatic.

I have also taken the opportunity to include some borders and images, beautifully painted by Julie Whitehouse, a Queensland artist. These will be valuable as resource material. These are also available in wrapping paper format, incorporating mirror images and repetition which will enhance your découpage projects — you can cut out borders, corners, a leaf here or there.

So consider the possibilities — create your own designs! And paint, paint, paint to your heart's content! That elusive title of 'artist' can be yours!

Nerida Singleton,
Brisbane 1996

Découpage Techniques

There are many styles of découpage, and just as many methods which can be pursued to produce a beautiful heirloom. Here we have given you instructions which suit a flat, hard surface, such as a wooden box, and alternative ways of working on a rounded project, such as a ceramic urn. The two techniques differ slightly in the sealing and gluing processes. Preparation, cutting, varnishing and polishing remain the same.

PREPARATION

(a) the surface

Your surface needs to be smooth before you begin assembling your cutouts into a beautiful design. Apply several coats of Gesso, if necessary, and lightly sand between coats until it is as smooth as marble. Gesso acts as a primer, filler and barrier. Paints and glues don't adhere well to surfaces such as metal, terracotta, glazed surfaces, plastics and vinyls, but an application of Gesso provides a barrier which allows adhesion. Irregular surfaces, such as those of ostrich and emu eggs, benefit from several coats of Gesso, as do old objects which have pitted surfaces. In these cases the Gesso acts as a filler and the surface can be sanded smooth.

Apply a sealer such as Liquitex Gloss Medium & Varnish (polymer medium) to already smooth objects, inside and out, to prevent glue seeping into a porous surface and thus to avoid losing adhesion between picture and object. (If you are employing Liquitex artist acrylic paints to your background, the sealer on top will not be necessary as these paints incorporate a binder or sealer in them — see introduction to painting backgrounds page 9).

Craftwood (M.D.F.) must be painted, Gessoed or sealed before sanding, as the dust particles contain formaldehyde, and workers should use a mask when sanding these products.

(b) the images

When you are using precious images, photographs or laser copies on a flat surface, they benefit from a sparing coat of sealer to protect the image from glue which may penetrate from behind, and from varnish which may penetrate from the top. Do this before you cut them out. The sealer provides a thin plastic film over the image and prevents a 'bleed' which will ruin your design. Be sure to be very sparing in your application of the sealer. It thickens paper and this can make fine cutting difficult. When working with very fine images, and if gluing to a rounded surface, sealing is unnecessary as you employ the sealer as a glue which effectively seals the image from behind. More sealer is applied to the completed design, so protecting the composition from the invasive varnish.

You can coat the back of an image which has print on the reverse, to prevent the print from showing through when the image is glued down. In such a case you should seal the front of the image, leave to dry, then mix equal quantities of Gesso and sealer and apply to the back of the image. Should you then be gluing directly on to a Gessoed surface, apply equal quantities of Gesso and sealer as a final coat, as the Gesso absorbs moisture from the glue and makes adhesion difficult.

You may prefer to spray a fixative to thin porous papers but be especially careful to do this with adequate ventilation as aerosols can be asphyxiating.

Do not attempt to seal images which have been cut out, as they will curl and stick to themselves.

CUTTING

Cut out your images using fine-tipped, curved cuticle or surgical scissors. The scissors should have fine tips with no air showing between the blades when viewed from the side. They should be fluid in their glide, and with comfortable grips. People are often frustrated with their cutting, but with a good pair of scissors their technique is vastly improved. When you are sure you will enjoy this art form, invest in the best pair of scissors which fit your budget.

Remember, fine cutting is crucial to the success of your composition.

When cutting, the curve of the scissor blades should point away from you to allow a crisp edge on the image. Cut interior unwanted background first. Poke a hole in from the top, then bring the scissors up from under the paper and cut out in a clockwise direction. All irrelevant background must be removed as it will show beneath the varnish.

For exterior cutting, feed the paper fluidly through the scissors, in an anticlockwise direction if right-handed. (The reverse applies to left-handed workers.) Cut away the most difficult area first while you have a substantial amount of paper to manipulate. You will find you are just using the tips of the scissors for fine cutting — about 2-3 mm (⅛ inch) — and your left hand is doing most of the work in feeding the paper through the scissors. Relax and enjoy this therapeutic exercise, ensuring you have good light.

DESIGNING YOUR COMPOSITION AND CHOOSING YOUR BACKGROUND

The choice of the focal image, which you love, will dictate all complementary images, and the appropriate background. The shape and line of this image will also determine what object you will choose to put it on. Obviously, a tall elongated image would not fit well on a fat, squat vase. Commonsense will help you in choosing your project.

Cut many more images than you need, because then you have options when constructing your design. Begin with your main (focal) image and Blu-tack it in place. Surround it with images of the same colour tones, adding and subtracting until you are pleased with the design. Leave your work for a time, and then look at the design from a distance, with no competing work around it. This allows you to be critical of your composition and it will be obvious to you whether it succeeds or fails. If you anguish over it and it seems that the composition is not coming together, get away from it altogether for a time. It will be more pleasurable when you are fresh.

Never decide upon the colour of your painted background until you are satisfied with your composition. This is one of two simple rules of découpage. The second is not to mix your colours on your palette as you will have a muddy effect, and no tonal variation in your colours. As this book concentrates on producing wonderful backgrounds for your découpage, full instructions for the painting techniques accompany each colour page.

Allow the background to dry overnight before gluing down your design.

GLUING

(a) rounded surfaces

When gluing onto a rounded surface you should employ a fine 00 brush and use it with the Liquitex Gloss Medium, gluing just a small area at one time. Begin at the widest part of your design, spread the medium generously behind the cutout and push the paper into place with your brush. Press down firmly with a damp piece of kitchen sponge. Continue this process until all the image is secured, working about a centimetre (half an inch) at a time.

If you are using a large image on a curved surface you may have to cut into the image to allow it to accommodate the curve without wrinkling and creasing. Some concave areas will overlay themselves, while convex areas will spread out, leaving background areas obvious. These will require retouching with your paints and a fine brush to disguise the areas which have been extensively cut. Choose a line on the image to cut, and be sure this line is the top-most when gluing down. Do not cut through faces, and glue the face down first to ensure you do no damage to it if the image creases.

Gently roll out excess glue with a rubber roller. You are trying to achieve an even distribution of glue behind the images, with no air pockets. Wipe any excess glue from the surface of your design.

(b) flat surfaces

Glue images one at a time, using a mixture of Clag and P.V.A. glue (4:1 mix) or wallpaper paste if you prefer. Apply the glue generously to the surface of the object. Rub the glue with your fingers until it is silky; remove any hard lumps; place the image on the glue with a small amount of glue on top to provide you with emulsion; lightly massage out air bubbles and excess glue using no pressure. Be careful though, because if you squeeze out all the glue there will be no adhesion with the picture, and the stress of the varnish will pull up blisters and air bubbles. When the glue has had time to bond to the surface you may lightly apply a rubber roller to the image, radiating out from the centre of the picture. Again, apply no pressure.

Wipe excess glue from the top of the picture (check for dull patches on the picture when held up to the light) using a damp sponge. Colour any white edges which may appear around the pictures with pencil. This shading allows the images to blend together.

Seal the composition sparingly, and repeat to protect the prints from the varnish. Allow 24 hours to dry.

VARNISHING

When varnishing, always work with a mask or respirator to guard against the hazards of varnish and turpentine fumes, and with goggles to protect your eyes. Your working environment should be well ventilated, dust free and with good light.

Do not varnish when the atmosphere is damp or excessively humid. It will take much longer to dry, and you run the risk of revarnishing over a damp coat, which can cause the surface to crackle — like crocodile skin if extreme.

Many applications of varnish will protect your composition and allow the images to glow through the depth of the varnish. However, you do not wish to bury or inter your prints.

Remove surface dust with a tack cloth before varnishing. Using a 2.5 cm (1 inch) imitation sable soft brush, apply successive coats of varnish evenly, a day apart, using the brush almost horizontally, and brushing in one direction (not back and forth as this will encourage air bubbles in the varnish). If you draw the brush through the varnish and apply it too thinly, you will notice definite bristle lines in your work. Float the varnish on your surface, merely using the brush to guide the varnish over the surface. Alter the direction of your stroke on subsequent applications, to ensure an even coverage in the crevices of your design.

Apply a good depth of varnish to protect your images (perhaps 20 coats).

Water-based varnishes, such as Cabot's Crystal Clear, allow a true clarity of colour on your design. Definitely do not use a foam brush when using water-based varnishes as they tend to incorporate air bubbles into your varnished surface. Oil-based varnishes, e.g. Estapol High Gloss, will mellow your work, and give it a glow which resembles an antique. You can 'set' your colour with a water-based varnish (perhaps 20 coats) then proceed with the oil-based one which provides a slightly ivory mellowness and is more durable. Do not attempt to do the reverse — if the background is becoming too mellow it is not possible to revert to water-based products. Water will not sit on oil. You will need to buy a new tin of varnish for more clear colour.

SANDING

After about twenty layers of varnish have been applied, and carefully dried, you can begin sanding. The objective here is to achieve an even surface, therefore we sand the images with a flat block, and do not sand down into the crevices within the design. These crevices will fill with successive varnish applications, and when the surface is completely dull after sanding you will have a flat, smooth surface.

After each sanding, apply another coat of varnish, dry completely, and sand again. You will require several coats of varnish and sandings between coats to achieve a smooth finish. The more the better!

Be sure to sand with a mask and goggles, and not in an enclosed space.

(a) water-based varnish
If you have used a water-based varnish, it is necessary to dry sand this product to avoid a cloudy or smoky look on your surface. Water-based varnishes are also much harder to sand, and a 280 SIA silicone carbide paper is the most effective.

(b) oil-based varnish
Oil-based varnishes can be wet or dry sanded, however 320 SIA will sand much more efficiently. This is a silicone impregnated dry paper which requires no water for emulsion.

Sand very lightly, using no pressure or you will scour your surface. It is far preferable to sand for a longer time than to exert pressure. Work in one direction, then the other (cross-hatched), and never sand in circles. Be sure to constantly rub the sandpaper through a rough towel to eliminate dust particles, and to remove the accumulated dust on the surface, too. Because this technique is superior and more efficient, you will use less varnish, fewer sandpapers, and much less effort in achieving your aim of a smooth finish.

If you prefer to wet sand, begin with a strip of 600 sandpaper around a rubber block, and, using a good amount of water, sand lightly in alternate directions. You will varnish and sand until the surface is smooth and uniformly dull, then, after a light sand with 1200 wet, apply several coats of varnish and leave for four weeks to cure. This method will aid the curing time and minimise the problems of moire taffeta waterwaves in the surface when you come to polish your project.

POLISHING

You can achieve a subtle sheen or a mirror shine on your finished object. Each surface requires the same preliminary steps. Lightly sand the surface, using 1200 wet around a foam block. You need to remove dust and gritty air bubbles only, and leave a matt surface. Work very lightly, as you do not wish to sand through the underlying coat. Wipe off any milky residue from your work and the sandpaper.

Then lightly rub over your surface with wet steel wool (No. 0000) to polish away any scratches. Use light friction and no power when doing this. Then apply a light film of beeswax to the steel wool, rub on to a small area at a time, buff immediately with lint-free fabric dipped in boiling water. Repeat this procedure until you achieve a mellow sheen to your work.

Micro-mesh is an alternative product which can be used confidently to achieve a satin finish or a mirror shine. It is available in a kit which contains grades of cushioned abrasive which move from 4000 to 6000, 8000 and 12000. Imagine how fine these are! The instructions lead you to cover the foam block with the 4000 sheet, and using it in the opposite direction to your 1200 wet sand, lightly rub over the surface with a plentiful amount of water. Continue sanding with the 4000 in alternate directions until the block slips over the surface. When it is active, it grabs the surface and you can hear the sound it makes. There are two 4000 papers in the kit as these do most of the work. Then, alternating the direction, move to the 6000, keeping the surface of the papers and object clean between applications. If you prefer a matt or low sheen, you can stop at this stage, or move through 8000, then 12000 for a higher shine.

CARE OF YOUR HEIRLOOM

Micro-mesh is a permanent finish, and simply requires a light rinse with warm, soapy water to restore it to a wonderful glow. Should your beeswax surface suffer from dust and grime, rub it with detergent and mineral turpentine (a few drops), then repolish it in the way described above to restore its subtle sheen.

Introduction to Painting Backgrounds

Winston Churchill began painting quite late in his life. He remembered the first day he tackled a blank canvas, a palette of assorted colours beside him. Where to begin? 'Well', he thought, 'the sky is blue!' and he dipped his brush firmly into the blue paint.

The successful painter never forgets that he or she was once right at the beginning, gazing helplessly at the tubes of paint.

Through our teaching of découpage, we have become very aware that this feeling of intimidation is a very common one. Hopefully, this book will dispel this uncertainty forever, and introduce you to the FUN of painting.

Much impossible-to-understand language has been written about this subject. We will give you a straightforward and simple guide so that you can begin to experiment with your paints to create your own individual backgrounds for your découpage images. It is this background that makes your completed work unique to you (the images, after all, can be used by others).

Before beginning, and just in case someone who is reading this would like a few essential facts about the paint, acrylic paint is the best medium to use with découpage. Any paint made from pigment bound in a synthetic resin is commonly known as an acrylic. It is stable and quick drying, and can be thinned or washed out with water. It dries as fast as water evaporates and once this happens, no further chemical reaction takes place. It is also a strong adhesive, each layer of paint gluing itself to the one underneath. The paint is opaque (a solid colour) but can be diluted with water to any kind of transparency. The rate of drying can be slowed with the addition of a retarder.

Acrylics are compatible with a wide variety of surfaces. They can be applied direct to the surface or onto an acrylic primer such as Gesso. There are two exceptions. Being water-suspended, they will not take over an oil-based ground. Also, if you are painting a pottery glazed surface (like an old vase) a coat of gesso is necessary first.

Painters using acrylics for the first time should experiment to discover which brands suit them best. There are subtle differences between certain brands. In this book, the brand used is Liquitex, for that is the brand we normally work with for many subtle reasons — e.g. the last drop squeezed from the tube is as fresh as the first one, and the pigment tones are very true and lasting. The paint is also a paste consistency, unlike some paints incorporating a flow medium specifically designed for folk art painting techniques. This paste consistency allows sponges to give a textured effect to your background.

Paint can be applied in just any way you feel comfortable working and if this means your fingers or a bit of rag, that's just fine. Everyone applies paint differently, so if you are experimenting with what we present here, and it doesn't seem to you to match up exactly, ask yourself this — 'Do I like it?'. And if you do, be content and happy as a sandcrab for you only have to please yourself!

In this book we have used only ONE technique with ONE implement — the sea sponge — and after you have mastered this you will feel you can do ANYTHING! We use it because it really is the simplest technique and one which can be mastered by anyone.

The most important element of découpage is the image. Choose one that you love, which is appropriate in shape. Then investigate the colours within the image and this will surely prompt you to consider an appropriate background. Then consider any other elements of design which can be added — e.g. borders, other complementary images, etc.

In the following pages we show how different backgrounds and different design elements can create quite different 'looks' for your work. Each image is repeated four times with four different background approaches (with the exception of the Christmas compositions). There is an accompanying hint of design in borders and other cut-out images, and through these it will become clear that there are many ways to change the character of your work. It will also become clear that it is the 'look' you desire which matters — not a set plan of what is right and wrong.

And you don't need a huge range of paints to create your desired effect. Artists mix up their own colours and you can, too, with a minimum of fuss.

Painting books often present a colour-wheel and heaps of technical terms. I have found that the quickest and most enjoyable way to see which colours make what is to select two colours, place one on a sheet of paper and push the other colour into it. By varying the amounts of each of the colours you will produce many variations and these are called 'tones'.

But it is important not to pre-mix the colour you want on your palette. Everyone wants to do this but it is a quick route to mud!, and you may as well just go down to the hardware store and buy a pot of paint that colour. If you take time to observe nature (even a leaf or a stick), you will see that no one tone of colour is the same all over because everything is affected by light (either moon, sun or man-made). The charm gained from a 'living' background is achieved with variations in tone, not one all-over colour. By adding one colour into another directly on to your work you will achieve different tones and have a feeling of light and shade that will bring life and sparkle to your work.

Val Lade,
Melbourne 1996

What You Will Need

....

TUBES OF PAINT

The Primary Colours are: red, yellow and blue. If you add white and black to your collection, just about any colour you can think of can be made.

Other colours used in this book are (all Liquitex Tubes):

Titanium White
Iridescent White
Iridescent Gold
Iridescent Copper
Burnt Umber
Hookers Green Deep
Cobalt Blue
Dioxazine Purple
Cadmium Yellow Medium
Napthol Crimson
Mars Black
Iridescent Bronze
Phthalocyanine Blue
Acra Violet
Phthalocyanine Green
Cadmium Red Medium

A PALETTE

A large WHITE ice-cream container lid is ideal for you need a flat surface. If you keep the container as well, throw in a piece of wet kitchen sponge (wettex) and then replace the lid you have been using and the paint will keep, preserved, for weeks. The paint does not slide off when upside down as it is a good paste consistency. It remains moist.

This is a home-made form of what is known as a 'wet palette'.

JAR OF WATER

Change this frequently as the water muddies.

A SPONGE

The best sort of sponge is a small sea sponge. They are sold in some art shops, but also chemist shops where they are sold for applying make-up. They are usually piled into a container. Go through them carefully and try and select one with the tightest holes in it. This will last longer.

The sea sponge holds the paint and water beautifully and gives an interesting texture to your work. Always wash it out thoroughly in running water after use — COLD water! Hot water will ruin it.

If you want to start painting immediately and don't have a sea-sponge, a square of thick household sponge will suffice but will not achieve quite the same textural effects.

WHITE PAPER

This is for testing your loaded sponge before applying it to your work or for taking paint off the sponge if you feel you have too much on it. A sketch pad is a useful purchase to experiment in and record colour combinations for later reference when you are looking for an appropriate background for an image.

Orchard Lady 1

....

A FEELING OF SUNSHINE IN THE ORCHARD

Colours:

Titanium White
Iridescent White
Iridescent Gold

1 Immerse the sea-sponge in cold water. Squeeze it almost dry.

2 Grasp the sponge with ALL fingers. You must feel in control of it as when you are holding a pen.

3 Scoop up a good heaped teaspoon of Titanium White on the base of the sponge and very quickly swirl in small circles, all over the paint surface. Immediately tap the sponge again all over the swirls to eliminate them and make the surface uniform. If the paint swirls have dried, add more white to your sponge. When tapping, barely lift the sponge from the surface and work very quickly.

4 Wash out the sponge in cold running water.

5 Leave paint to dry for 30 minutes.

6 Using Iridescent White, repeat the method described in 3. You will find, however, that you will need to use more paint as the Iridescent White is translucent. Like a good cook, one must be generous with the ingredients!

7 Without stopping to remove any remains of Iridescent White from the sponge, delve into a good dollop of Iridescent Gold and pat and drag it in different directions over the wet Iridescent White, leaving spaces of pure white showing through. Make sure the sponge travels in different directions when you are applying this. Turn your wrist constantly.

8 Leave to dry. Rinse out the sponge, and if the paint is all used, clean palette under running water with a nail brush.

Orchard Lady 2

....

A FEELING OF THE WOOD OF THE TREES

Colours:

Burnt Umber
Iridescent White
Irisescent Copper
Iridescent Gold

1 Scoop up equal quantities of Burnt Umber and Iridescent White onto the sponge together — about a heaped teaspoonful at a time. Pat and push both colours onto the surface so they mix in as you go.

2 Dry for 30 minutes. Rinse out the sponge.

3 Now scoop up equal quantities of Iridescent White, copper and gold all together. Firmly push the loaded sponge down on the palette to distribute the paint into the sponge. Give a good strong push several times. Test now on the white paper that you don't have great lumps of any of the colours left. Push and pat the sponge (barely lifting it from the surface at any time) over the dried paint. These soft tones lighten the original darkish background and bring it to life. If, by any chance, you find you've left a spot of any of the colours you don't want, just push the sponge back over it.

4 Dry. Clean sponge and palette.

Orchard Lady 3

························

THE GREEN GRASS AND EARTH OF THE ORCHARD

Colours:

Hookers Green
Iridescent Copper

(N.B. Make sure your tube of Hookers Green does not read 'Hookers Green Hue'. It is a much lighter shade and 'Hookers Green' is a very dark, almost 'black/green' colour.)

1 Scoop Hookers Green and Iridescent Copper together onto sponge and work all over the surface. This is known as 'wet into wet', i.e. two different colours blending at the same time. What amounts of each colour you use is up to you. Some might like to accent more copper than I have. Just keep adding different amounts of both until you are satisfied.

2 Dry.

3 Rinse out sponge and palette.

Orchard Lady 4

··

EMPHASIS ON THE PURPLE GRAPES AND GREEN LEAVES AND CAPTURING THE MOUNTAINS

Colours:

Iridescent Gold
Cobalt Blue
Dioxazine Purple

1 Scoop Iridescent Gold and Cobalt Blue together onto the sponge. Pat and push upwards these colours so that they form a soft green.

2 While the above is still wet, add scattered dabs (about 7.5cm or 3 inches apart) of Dioxazine Purple. Don't get a fright about how dark it is. Just turn the sponge to a clean moist part and rub the dark purple briskly until it merges with the gentle green you have made.

3 Dry.

4 Rinse out sponge and palette.

Japanese Lady 1

A PEACEFUL, DELICATE SOLUTION

Colours:

Cobalt Blue
Acra Violet
Iridescent White

1 (Exception to the rule!) Mix Cobalt Blue with two pinheads of Acra Violet on the palette. Pick up this colour onto the sponge with some Iridescent White and pat all over.

2 Dry five minutes or until it is still damp but not heavily wet.

3 Load the sponge with Iridescent White and drag the sponge at an angle through the damp blue to give a hint of the steam from the pot.

4 Dry.

5 Rinse out sponge and palette.

Japanese Lady 2

FOCUSSING ON THE NECK TRIM

Colours:

Acra Violet
Iridescent Copper
Iridescent White

1 Scoop up on the sponge Acra Violet and Iridescent Copper together. Push and pat over surface firmly. This will be quite rich in colour.

2 Dry for 30 minutes.

3 Clean sponge.

4 Load two heaped teaspoonsful of Iridescent White onto the sponge and rub and pat briskly all over the underpaint so that the colour is softened.

5 Dry.

6 Clean sponge and palette.

Japanese Lady 3

The feel of silk

Colours:

Iridescent Bronze
Iridescent Gold

1 Scoop Iridescent Gold and Iridescent Bronze onto sponge together. Pat and work both colours all over surface so that there is a variation of tone. Don't be hesitant to pick up just one of the colours again from your palette and highlight it in different areas. You are in charge, and can do just what you like. The only criterion is that you like it.

2 Dry.

3 Clean sponge and palette

Japanese Lady 4

....

THE BIRD CALLS FOR A STRONG APPROACH

Colours:

Phthalocyanine Green
Iridescent Copper
Iridescent White

1 Scoop Phthalocyanine Green and Iridescent Copper together onto sponge. Work them wet into wet, adding more of both to get a good strong dark tone.

2 As the above paint is beginning to dry take some Iridescent White on a clean sponge and work it lightly on top of the other paint from the middle outwards so that it will back the central image and carry through the feel of the floating steam.

3 Dry.

4 Clean sponge and palette.

Black and White Water Nymph 1

WATER AND SEAWEED ILLUSION

Colours:

Cobalt Blue
Iridescent Gold

1 Work Cobalt Blue and gold together on the sponge. Pat quickly all over and then add a bit more Iridescent Gold over again. Do not work and pat too long or you will lose the patches of pure blue and gold. Some of it will have the green look of the cutouts around the image. That will be where the gold and cobalt blue have seriously intermingled.

2 Dry.

3 Rinse out sponge and palette.

Black and White Water Nymph 2

···

THE BINDWEED GROWS AT THE WATER'S EDGE AND IS HELD BY THE CHILD

Colours:

Iridescent Bronze
Dioxazine Purple

1 Swirl and pat a solid colour of bronze all over.

2 Dry for 30 minutes.

3 Scoop bronze and Dioxazine Purple in equal quantities onto sponge. Pat gently over the bronze background until both colours are softly merged.

4 Dry.

5 Clean sponge and palette.

Black and White Water Nymph 3

··

THE CLIFF ELEMENT

Colours:

Iridescent Bronze
Iridescent Copper

1 Scoop both colours, in equal quantities onto the sponge.
Pat on gently, leaving some of the white background showing
through to give a hint of the cliff structure in the image.

2 Dry.

3 Clean sponge and palette.

Black and White Water Nymph 4

....

A SUBTLE MOVEMENT AWAY FROM BLACK AND WHITE

Colours:

Mars Black
Titanium White
Napthol Crimson
Iridescent White
Iridescent Gold

1 Swirl and pat Mars Black all over surface.

2 While it is still wet pat Titanium White, then crimson over the black.

3 Dry for 30 minutes.

4 Push Iridiscent White firmly into the texture of the sponge and rub briskly and quickly over all the paintwork.

5 As the Iridescent White was rubbed on, it will be dry almost immediately. Without cleaning up the sponge, pick up Iridescent Gold on it and also rub that over briskly.

6 Dry.

7 Clean sponge and palette.

Chiffon Lady 1

·····································

A CHARACTER ANALYSIS

Colours:

**Cadmium Yellow Medium,
Iridescent Copper,
Acra Violet,
Burnt Umber**

1 Swirl and pat Cadmium Yellow all over smoothly.

2 Dry for 30 minutes.

3 Scoop Acra Violet and copper together onto the sponge and pat all over allowing the yellow to show through every now and then.

4 While this is still wet, add Burnt Umber to the sponge and pat through the paint lightly, going back over more darkly around the edges. Even around the edges, still allow the yellow to show through.

5 Dry.

6 Clean sponge and palette.

Chiffon Lady 2

A SOFT BUT FIRM CONTRAST TO THE DELICACY
OF THE IMAGE

Colours:

Iridescent Copper
Iridescent Bronze

1 Swirl and pat a coat of bronze all over.

2 Dry for 30 minutes.

3 Scoop up slightly more copper than bronze together on the
sponge. Pat all over the dried bronze, making sure there is
enough domination of copper to glow and pick up the flesh
tones of the image.

4 Dry.

5 Clean sponge and palette.

Chiffon Lady 3

....

A HINT OF RICH VELVET

Colours:

Acra Violet
Iridescent Gold
Iridescent Copper
Iridescent Bronze

1 Swirl and pat a coat of Acra Violet all over.

2 Dry for 30 minutes.

3 Pat gold lightly over.

4 While above is still wet, pat copper all over.

5 The gold and copper are still wet, so now add the bronze gently. Allow the Acra Violet to show through each time.

6 Dry.

7 Clean sponge and palette.

Chiffon Lady 4

....

A CONTINUATION OF THE BACKGROUND OF THE IMAGE

Colours:

Dioxazine Purple
Hookers Green
Iridescent Gold
Acra Violet

1 Swirl and pat Dioxazine Purple all over.

2 Dry for 30 minutes.

3 Pat Hookers Green all over the purple.

4 While wet, add gold and Acra Violet on top of and into the Hookers Green.

5 Dry.

6 Clean sponge and palette.

Taffetta Lady 1

································

A THREE DIMENSIONAL LOOK, PICKING UP THE TAFFETA COLOUR

Colours:

Dioxazine Purple
Mars Black
Iridescent Gold

1 Scoop ⅞ths of purple and ⅛th of black onto sponge and work all over background. Too much black will eliminate the purple shade.

2 Dry until still faintly tacky.

3 With a water-laden sponge mix on the palette a wash (consistency of milk) of gold and purple. Test it onto the white paper first to make sure it is well mixed onto the sponge. Using a delicate touch, pat this mixture all over the existing purple and black.

4 Dry.

5 Clean sponge and palette.

Taffetta Lady 2

....

A MORE DELICATE APPROACH PICKING UP
THE ROCK COLOUR

Colours:

Titanium White
Iridescent White
Acra Violet
Iridescent Gold

1 Swirl and pat Titanium White all over for a smooth
background.

2 While this is still wet, pat Iridescent White and a pinhead
of Acra Violet all over.

3 Again while still wet, add touches of gold.

4 Add more gold all around the edges.

5 Dry.

Taffetta Lady 3

···

THE DARK GREEN SHADOWS CAPTURED

Colours:

Hookers Green
Iridescent Copper

1 Swirl and pat Hookers Green all over until smooth
and dark.

2 Dry for 30 minutes.

3 Collect Hookers Green and copper in equal quantities onto
the sponge. Push the sponge and colours firmly downwards
onto the palette to immerse the paint into the texture of the
sponge. Pat gently and quickly all over the dried
Hookers Green.

4 Dry.

5 Clean sponge and palette.

Taffetta Lady 4

A REMINDER OF THE ROSE

Colours:

Napthol Crimson
Dioxazine Purple
Iridescent Gold
Cobalt Blue
Iridescent White

1 Rub and pat a coat of crimson all over. Looks quite shockingly bright but do not worry!

2 Dry for 30 minutes.

3 With a sponge loaded with water, push into it a dot of Dioxazine Purple and push and mix it on the palette into a pale purple wash. Pat this all over the dried crimson.

4 Dry for 30 minutes.

5 Make another wash of Cobalt Blue and sponge it all over.

6 Dry for 30 minutes.

7 A wash of gold, lightly done, all over.

8 Dry for 30 minutes.

9 Rub a teaspoonful of Iridescent White over all your paintwork. If it still looks too strong a colour overall, just repeat this last step again until you are satisfied.

10 Dry.

11 N.B. You have worked right through from dark to quite light in this exercise. The processes give it a particular depth.

12 Clean sponge and palette.

Madonna and Child

....

**A RICH RENAISSANCE APPROACH TO
HERALD THE SEASON**

Colours:

**Iridescent Gold
Cadmium Red Medium
Iridescent Bronze**

1 Swirl and pat a coat of Iridescent Gold all over until a smooth even sheen.

2 Dry for 30 minutes.

3 Scoop up on sponge ⅔ Iridescent Gold and ⅓ Cadmium Red together. Pat all over dried gold.

4 While this is still wet, sponge Iridescent Bronze around all the outside edges, curving the corners.

5 Dry.

6 Clean sponge and palette.

Christmas Angel

....

FLIGHT IN A CHRISTMAS SKY

Colours:

Cadmium Red
Phthalocyanine Green
Iridescent Gold

1 Sponge gold heavily in the middle section only first.

2 Dry for 30 minutes.

3 With a saltspoon of Cadmium Red to a teaspoonful of Iridescent Gold together on a sponge, return firstly to inner area of dried gold and pat gently, followed by a stronger and more dense colour around the outer circle of gold. Still leave the outer edges free.

4 While all this is still wet, pick up on the sponge (which is still carrying remainder of red and gold in it) some Phthalocyanine Green. Sponge this firmly into the outer edges of the circle (where you will have quite strong Cadmium Red and gold colour), and the rest of the areas on the perimeter. Keep sponging until it all blends well from colour to colour.

5 While the above is all still wet, sponge gold again by itself over the whole area.

6 Dry.

7 N.B. If any areas seem too dark or dominant to you, just add a light colour and the reverse for covering too light an area.

8 Clean sponge and palette.

For further details on découpage techniques and projects please read our other books:

Lade, Val. *Eighteenth Century Découpage, The Definitive Guide*, Milner, Sydney 1994.

Singleton, Nerida. *Découpage An Illustrated Guide*, Milner, Sydney, 1991.

— *Découpage Project Kit Book*, Milner, Sydney,1994.